I0536283

Eat Bananas with a Spoon

Unpeel Life's Lessons with Bite-size Inspirations

Riya Aarini

ISBN: 978-1-956496-57-4 (Paperback)
ISBN: 978-1-956496-58-1 (eBook)

www.riyapresents.com

Contents

Happiness

Tune out the noise of the world, listen to your heart, and the music of life plays beautifully.

Out of nothing, winners create positive life experiences. Out of nothing, complainers create negative life experiences.

Of all the thoughts you could possibly think, why not think good ones?

Happiness is a topic worthy of discussing, but even more worthy of feeling.

Contentment is a way of life. Everyone is gifted with the power to be content, if not ridiculously satisfied.

If you intend to reap a harvest of joy and contentment, till your own plot of land—not your neighbor's.

It takes a lifetime to realize human potential. Self-knowledge still remains incomplete. Despite its fathomlessness, the human spirit yearns to be explored from its boundless depths to its heights.

A wealthy oil tycoon resides in a gorgeous mansion with a ten-car garage filled with exotic sports cars, suffers a beautiful two-timing mistress, and wears flashy designer suits to his high-stress job. But the mogul's plumber adores his faithful wife, drives a twelve-year-old truck, and enjoys the company of his jovial friends. He performs an honest day's work in overalls, and is happier than the millionaire whose toilet he plunges.

Meaning

Happiness is fleeting, but meaning is steadfast.

When you write a poem that touches the heart of another, you've inspired a lovely sentiment in a place where that lovely sentiment was not before.

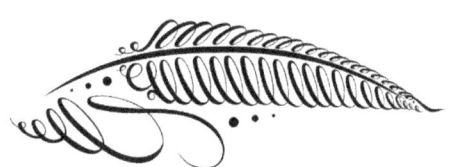

Meaning is accompanied by deep and lasting joy. But happiness is largely devoid of meaning. The wisest know the difference—and strive for meaning.

When you grow up, that pudgy elementary school teacher with the silly snort-sneeze who encouraged you to chase your dreams is more fondly remembered than last year's size-two beauty pageant winner.

The world glimmers with hope. If you cannot see it or hear it, you can feel it to know it.

Love

Loving is an art, and we are all gifted painters capable of producing a masterpiece.

When someone loves you with all their heart, asking for more is like wanting to win the lottery a second time.

Love is filled with such beauty that it breaks your heart, allowing more love to enter.

Control is the flightless bird. Love is the soaring eagle.

To innocent lovers, sweet nothings mean everything.

Love delightfully fools us into believing what a wonderful world we live in.

When it comes to love, what is there to say that feelings could not describe better?

Love is no ordinary emotion. Love makes your heart soar. It is the wind behind a kite that climbs to the loftiest heights.

Time slowly cools the hot coals of anger, but it is love that pours over them and extinguishes their heat instantly.

Love is a cool drink in the parched desert of life.

Love is the elixir of life.

The purpose of life is to love—and if you're lucky, to be loved.

Love speaks to the spirit, gently persuading it to give to others the precious gift it receives. It's not a selfish emotion, but one that gives eternally.

Love is life's guiding light. We are all inexperienced seafarers sailing our boats in the ocean of life. When the storm hits, it's love that calms us and allows us to navigate with clarity.

Love flourishes in humility.

Romantic love is canny and unwilling to be shortchanged. Ask any lonesome fool.

Love cracks the tough nutshell and softly touches the tender kernel inside.

Humanity is graciously offering to others the loving words you longed for someone to offer you.

Death

Life is colored by seasons: a season of health, a season of sickness, a season of gain, a season of loss, a season of peace, a season of turmoil. Like spring follows winter, the next season is always around the bend.

Death is a merited graduation from life. It is an occasion for satisfaction that one has literally and figuratively passed.

Life is a song you write and perform, and the people you touch never get your heart-rending music out of their heads.

Friendship

Friendship bonds are gifts of life that take untiring effort to create and yet are impossible to break.

The messages most heard are those that flow directly into our hearts.

Those who prize a fellowship with humanity value a tolerance for folly.

For the few, our best friends are philosophers who spoke unparalleled wisdom millennia ago. But for the many, good books are friends who understand an aching heart better than people do.

Some people exude such genuine warmth of humanity that being in their presence is a precious experience.

Loneliness

Even the lonely are connected. There's a beautiful feeling of connection between those whose hearts are broken to the same degree.

When faced with rejection from every angle, remember that special someone loves you, and feel peace in your heart. And if you don't have a special someone, remember that special pet who relies on you. And if you don't have a special someone or a special pet, remember that the Creator loves you. And if you don't believe in a Creator . . . be kind to someone, and rejoice in humanity.

Pain

Saving someone drowning in despair involves taking a deep breath, diving to meet them in the depths of their darkness, and pulling them back to the light of the surface. It's an extraordinary task reserved for extraordinary people.

Great pain, when mixed with deep introspection, leads to great wisdom.

Unaddressed pain is like dust. You sweep it under the rug, but it lingers, drifting out at the most inopportune moments, polluting the air you breathe, and being the invisible cause of miserable sickness.

Share your load with a magnanimous soul who's willing to help you carry it.

The materialists applaud those who spread joy—
but the spiritualists embrace those who seek joy.

Traveling the flat plains is an easy, uninspiring journey. It is vigorously climbing the steep hills and perilously descending the frightening valleys that give life its stimulating richness.

Power

Social status is a product of the active imagination. High-ranking politicians and royals aren't beneath wiping their noses either.

Explaining yourself further and further is like sinking deeper and deeper into quicksand. This is why politicians are knee-deep.

It's an enigma that celebrities are grossly overrated, and good, ordinary people are highly underrated.

When you're on the top of the world, one slip, and it's a long way down.

Charity

The most charitable deeds are performed by the unpretentious. They are society's nameless undercover agents, working clandestinely to elevate humankind.

Genuine actions speak to the heart as powerfully as they speak from the heart.

Sometimes the hand that gives does not fully understand the boundless impacts of its charity.

Good deeds are similar to floodwater. The benevolence trickles into nooks and crannies, saturating even the inconspicuous places with goodwill.

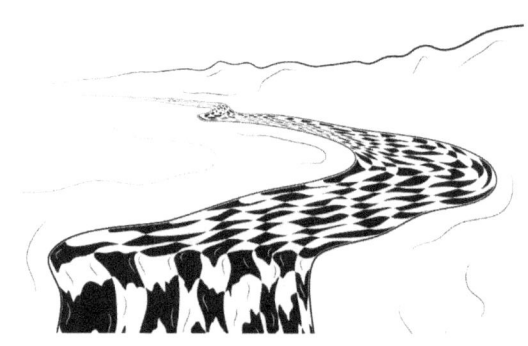

Life is a television show in which you enjoy a starring role—later generations never fail to replay your most memorable moments.

Success

Success is a prize most earnestly sought. We never tire of seeking success, because she never fails to entice us.

Some people earn a few meager dollars, yet are so rich in humanity that they are wealthier than the most prosperous millionaires.

Successful folks aren't the only ones entitled to a good life.

Earthly pleasures, from fragrant lavender gardens to breathtaking mountain views, give life its intrigue. None of life's commonplace joys demand a prior visit from success.

There are two kinds of people in the world: producers and consumers. Consumers consume the great things producers produce, and producers produce the great things consumers consume.

You do not own success. Success owns you.

No one can predict success or failure; if anyone could, the recipe for the former would be mass produced and distributed to all corners of the Earth.

The secret to success is simple. Anyone who wishes to be successful in the world of people needs only to connect with the people of the world. The secret sauce to success is connection.

To fruit success, connection must be genuine. Mix together one part authenticity and one part connection. Like a no-fail custard, this time-tested recipe holds form.

Worthy accomplishments aren't handed to us on a silver platter. The hungry are tasked with performing the laborious work to savor the experience of fine cuisine.

Success comes in various guises. The world reveres showy material success, but humble individuals hold unassuming personal success dear. No one needs permission to bask in its quiet serenity.

Use this flawless hack to manifest success in your life: set the bar low, and you'll always be a success.

All success is not equal. The most worthwhile
success is being kind.

Some folks make their fortune by following the book. Others make their fortune by writing the book.

Fickle success is never faithful. One day she favors you. The next day she abandons you.

Success can be bad to do business with, because she offers no guarantees—no matter your investment in time, energy, or effort.

Success and failure are illusions, perspectives developed by the supple mind. The enormously successful feel like miserable failures, and the worst failures feel like wild successes.

When you leave your small part of the world a better place, you've succeeded more than words can say.

Failure

Failure does not necessarily rob life of joy.

Failure can be a valuable friend—bestowing life lessons and enrichment.

Failure is a compass with a magnetic needle that points you in the right direction, or a street sign that indicates you're in the wrong lane. To those who are lost, either is incredibly valuable.

Some people's entire lives teeter precariously on a mere letter or a trivial number. There's more to life than an A or an F, or a one hundred or a zero.

Being number one is not always most desirable. Society needs numbers two, three, ten, fifty, and so on. Where would we be without the one hundred and the three hundred thousand?

Failure succeeds in giving rise to character—resilience, perseverance, determination—not even success advances character with such vigor.

The struggle for excellence is so enriching that
the effort itself is a success.

There's only one straight path to failure—and that is neglecting to try.

A life is not defined by many failures, but by a lifetime of valorous attempts.

The key to success lies in keeping up the good efforts with equally good spirits. What have you got to lose? You've got an entire lifetime to keep at it.

When everyone's on top of the world, success loses its appeal.

Living the life of your dreams is the fruit of careful self-examination, resourcefulness, and the courage to put the gears into motion.

Success may come with bargains you never planned for.

Self-worth

It's not success that creates self-value.

It's self-value that creates success.

Obstacles force you to slow down from life's hectic pace and appreciate its unending beauty.

Many unhappy people are gifted actors, putting on a show of happiness for the world.

We are all glorious pearls nestled in oysters, formed and beautified by life's irritating grains of sand.

There are those who are bought and know not that they are bought. There are those who are free and know that they are free.

It is not the sea that defines the shore but its own composition. Just so, it is not the sea of people that defines you but the actions inspired by your own heart.

Low self-worth is a malignant disease, silently spreading and destroying every irreplaceable moment of precious life. Once you realize you are stricken, make haste to cure yourself.

Be kind, not only to others, but to yourself. Unreplenished kindness is an empty reservoir that's too dry to dip from. When you give kindness to yourself, you instantly increase your reserves to give kindness to others.

When lending a helping hand to others, do not forget to lend one to yourself.

Within all of us, whether we know it or not, is an inborn self-respect.

The ability to love others falls in direct proportion to the ability to love yourself.

The wildflowers reaching toward the sky from the dusty side of the road are as exquisite and fragrant as the bouquet of cultivated roses arranged perfectly in a fine crystal vase.

A pauper without a penny to his name owns a heart of gold. Yet a wealthy man possesses a heart of stone. Who is truly rich?

We care not whether a man is rich or poor, whether a woman is beautiful or homely, or whether either is powerful or weak. All we care about is the dignity they show us.

The lost search the starry skies for answers, but the found search their own hearts.

Listen to your feelings, because they are the lighthouse in a stormy sea. Mistrust rattles the nerves like an alarm warning of danger. Trust calms the spirit, beckoning it to safety. You might avoid a shipwreck!

A sixty-year-old feels like a nimble twenty-year-old trapped in a wrinkled body. We never feel as old as our appearance betrays.

Life

Nothing lasts, not the sunlight through the trees,
not the twinkle of the stars, not the curses, not
the blessings, not the melancholy, not the cheer.
The fleeting nature of life can be a saving grace.

Life consists of three unanswered questions.

Life begins with, 'How did I get here?'

Life progresses to, 'Why am I here?'

Life ends with, 'When am I leaving?'

Life is such that, not infrequently, we want to escape for a while.

To get to where you want to be, you must know where you are.

Sometimes, here is no better place to be lost.

Life is a sport with a lot of rules. Those who brazenly ignore the playbook are kicked out of the game.

When everything goes wrong and out of control all at once, it feels like a sophisticated setup orchestrated by life itself.

Some lives are filled with wrong turns. But during the confusing ride, you see a side of the world you otherwise never see, and you discover a resilience you otherwise never discover.

You innocently make plans, but life trumps them with its own impromptu plans. It catches you off guard—if not this time, the next. Life is confusing, uncertain, and unpredictable—a true adventure.

It's hard to keep control of the reins on the chariot of life. Feisty horses and perilous routes give rise to sore tumbles. The determined charioteers dust themselves off, climb back on, and seize the reins again.

Life is a beautiful mix of relationships, conversations, and actions. Relationships are enjoyable when you feel good things. Conversations are enjoyable when you speak good things. Life is enjoyable when you do good things.

Pithy words are fluff.

Pithy words put into moral actions are substance.

The misfits, the eccentrics, the quirky—we're all guests in a world that doesn't belong to us.

Nature is an awesome power that not only amazes you, but shakes you, whips you, and sends you to the brink of death, until you show it unwavering respect.

Ignorance is most dangerous when it mistakenly thinks it's wise.

Every life is a story. Every day is a paragraph in the story. Every hour is a carefully selected word in the incredible making of the life story.

On life's journey, knowledge is a worthwhile companion.

Life provides the open-minded with answers they did not know they were searching for.

Hold regular conversations with truth, and open the closed gates of your heart and mind.

Every life is an expendable pawn in the Creator's magnificent game—yet each is a vital piece without which the Creator couldn't play.

Experts of existence, specialists of living, and connoisseurs of life are imposters. Life changes course daily, and we wake up trying to find a better way—reconfirming that none of us have it mastered. We are all perpetual amateurs.

Life is a carpenter that will sand you down until you are no longer rough around the edges, but a smooth and glistening sculpture, worthy of respect.

Enough is what should be seen when you look in the mirror.

If you teach a child a lesson in kindness, you've made not-so-little gains for humankind.

Evil assails our world. When wrongdoers intrude, do not become evil too.

Life doesn't have any stops. It just keeps going at full speed. The most prepared buckle up for the ride.

One's capacity for sadness is equal to one's capacity for happiness. Those who feel deep sorrow are capable of profound joy. It's the same cup that holds either gladness or gloom.

The broken pot lets in the light. Everyone is broken to a degree, meaning everyone is capable of letting in at least a sliver of light.

We're all in the race of life. But who speeds to the finish line? Those who love life leisurely walk, taking in the sights, the smells, the sounds, the feels of exquisite life.

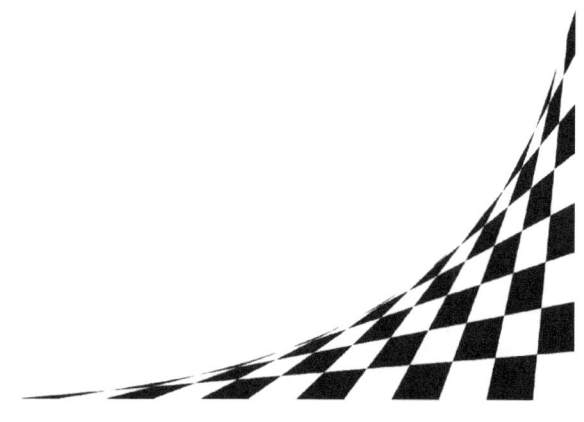

There is a time to acquire wisdom, and a time to put it into practice.

For the broken, living another day should earn them a badge of honor.

Sometimes we feel at peace not knowing, and that is plenty.

Life is an untiring teacher. We persist as life's continual students, whether we feel we know it all at twenty-one, or realize we know nothing at all at one hundred and one.

Home is a place we carry within ourselves.

Thank you for reading
Eat Bananas with a Spoon: Unpeel Life's
Lessons with Bite-size Inspirations.
Your honest thoughts about this book are
appreciated. Please consider leaving a review!

www.riyapresents.com